D1308890

POLAR REGIONS

Paul Mason

A⁺
Smart Apple Media

GEOGRAPHY FACT FILES

COASTLINES

DESERTS

MOUNTAINS

OCEANS

POLAR REGIONS

RIVERS

First published in 2004 by Hodder Wayland

338 Euston Road, London NW1 3BH, United Kingdom

Hodder Wayland is an imprint of Hodder Children's
Books, a division of Hodder Headline Limited. This
edition published under license from Hodder Children's
Books. All rights reserved.

Produced for Hodder Wayland by

Monkey Puzzle Media Ltd

Gissing's Farm, Fressingfield, Suffolk IP21 5SH

United Kingdom

Copyright © 2004 Hodder Wayland

Editor	Nicola Edwards
Designer	Jamie Asher
Picture Researcher	Sally Cole
Illustrator	Michael Posen
Consultant	Michael Allaby

Published in the United States by Smart Apple Media

2140 Howard Drive West

North Mankato, Minnesota 56003

U.S. publication copyright © 2005 Smart Apple Media
International copyright reserved in all countries. No part
of this book may be reproduced in any form without
written permission from the publisher.
Printed in China

Library of Congress Cataloging-in-Publication Data

Mason, Paul, 1967–
Polar regions / by Paul Mason.
p. cm. — (Geography fact files)
ISBN 1-58340-428-7
1. Polar regions—Juvenile literature. I. Title. II. Series.

G587.M38 2004

919.8—dc22   2004042919

9 8 7 6 5 4 3 2 1

Acknowledgements

We are grateful to the following for permission to
reproduce photographs: Alamy 35 top (Brian Atkinson);
Bryan and Cherry Alexander *back cover left*, 1 (Steve
Pinfield), 3 top and middle, 4, 6, 9 top, 10 both, 11
(Steve Pinfield), 13 bottom, 14, 15, 16 (Steve Pinfield),
17, 18, 19, 21, 26, 27 top, 28, 29, 31 top, 36, 37, 42,
44; Corbis 25 bottom (Bettmann), 38 (Natalie Fobes), 39
(Caroline Penn); Getty Images *front cover* (Art Wolfe);
Mary Evans Picture Library 23; Nature Picture Library 3
bottom (Martha Holmes), 33 (Martha Holmes), 34 (Mike
Salisbury), 43 bottom (Staffan Widstrand); Old
Dartmouth Historical Society, New Bedford Whaling
Museum 20; Popperfoto.com 24, 25 top; Science Photo
Library 30 (British Antarctic Survey); Still Pictures 8 (Anne
Piantanida), 12 (Klein/Hubert), 13 top (Juan Carlos
Munoz), 32 (J J Alcalay), 35 bottom (Gunter Ziesler), 41
(Anne Piantanida), 43 top (Hartmut Schwarzbach), 45
(Emmanuel Jeanjean); Werner Forman Archive 22 (The
Greenland Museum).

Title page picture: Adult emperor penguins shelter their
chicks from a blizzard in Antarctica.

CONTENTS

WHAT ARE POLAR REGIONS?

Imagine a land so cold that few living creatures can survive. It has no visible plants, animals, or human inhabitants. All that's there is a desert-like expanse of snow and ice, with perhaps a few rocky outcrops. These lands do exist beyond imagination, at the heart of the world's polar regions.

SIMILARITIES AND DIFFERENCES

The polar regions lie around the North and South Poles. They share common characteristics, most obviously a harsh, freezing-cold climate that makes living at the poles themselves almost impossible (though a scientific research station is kept at the South Pole). But there are also important differences between the northern and southern polar regions.

Deep beneath the ice of the South Pole is a landmass, the continent of Antarctica. Antarctica expands and contracts its area depending on the time of year: the shelf of ice around its coast shrinks in summer and grows bigger during winter. But at all times, Antarctica is surrounded by the barrier of the Southern Ocean.

A fishing settlement in Newfoundland, Canada.

The Arctic region is defined in different ways: by latitude (the Arctic Circle), temperature (the 50 °F [10 °C] isotherm), and vegetation (the treeline).

The North Pole and the Arctic regions that surround it are sited on the thick ice of the Arctic Ocean. No landmass lies beneath the ice. Instead, the Arctic is surrounded by the northern edges of three continents: North America, Europe, and Asia. People from these continents have lived on the fringes of the Arctic for centuries.

FACT FILE

THE FIVE NORTH POLES

There is more than one North Pole! (In this book, "North Pole" refers to the north geographic pole.)

• THE NORTH GEOGRAPHIC POLE lies near the center of the Arctic Ocean, where all of Earth's lines of longitude meet.

• THE INSTANTANEOUS NORTH POLE lies at the point where Earth's axis meets the surface. Earth wobbles slowly as it turns around its axis, so the instantaneous pole moves. It travels clockwise around an irregular path called the Chandler Circle.

• THE NORTH POLE OF BALANCE lies at the center of the Chandler Circle. Its position locates the north geographic pole. Each year since 1900, the north pole of balance has moved about six inches (15 cm) toward North America.

• THE NORTH MAGNETIC POLE is the farthest point on Earth in the direction of magnetic north. This pole can move many miles in a few years.

• THE GEOMAGNETIC NORTH POLE lies in Greenland. In Earth's upper atmosphere, the magnetic field points toward this point.

50 °F (10 °C) isotherm

Treeline

Alaska

Russia

Canada

North Geographic Pole

Greenland

Arctic Circle

Europe

DEFINING POLAR REGIONS

The edges of the areas called "polar regions" can be defined in several ways. One is to use a map that shows both the Arctic and Antarctic Circles. These lie 66 degrees and 30 minutes north and south of the equator, and about 1,620 miles (2,613 km) from the respective poles. The circles mark the farthest point at which the sun theoretically stays in the sky for 24 hours at midsummer, and doesn't rise at all for 24 hours at midwinter.

Another way of defining polar regions is based on climate. In the Arctic, for example, scientists have recorded the point at which the average summer temperature is 50 °F (10 °C). This line is known as the 50 °F (10 °C) isotherm, and can be used to mark the edge of the polar lands.

The 50 °F (10 °C) isotherm coincides with another defining point for Arctic lands: the treeline. This is the northernmost point at which trees can grow; farther north, the short growing season and freezing temperatures mean trees cannot survive.

THE ARCTIC

U nlike the South Pole, which is above land, the North Pole lies over the sea. A thick, permanent layer of ice known as the polar ice cap separates any explorer standing at the Pole from the ocean. This ice cap changes its size, growing larger in winter as more ice freezes in the cold temperatures, then shrinking in summer as higher temperatures lead to a thaw.

ISLANDS AND CONTINENTS

In places, the ice cap touches the lands that surround the Arctic Ocean (see map on page 5). Northern parts of the U.S., Canada, Norway, Sweden, Finland, and Russia all have territories that fringe the Arctic. There are also several groups of islands in the region, especially around the top of North America.

 **FACT FILE**

THE ARCTIC OCEAN

The Arctic Ocean is the smallest of the world's five oceans (after the Pacific, Atlantic, Indian, and Southern Oceans).

• LOCATION The body of water between Europe, Asia, and North America, mostly north of the Arctic Circle

• AREA Total: 5.6 million square miles (14 million sq km)

• COASTLINE 28,141 miles (45,389 km)

• LOWEST POINT Fram Basin, -15,301 feet (-4,665 m) (highest: sea level, zero feet [0 m])

• NATURAL RESOURCES Sand and gravel aggregates, mineral deposits, polymetallic nodules, oil and gas fields, fish, marine mammals (seals and whales)

• ENVIRONMENTAL ISSUES Endangered marine species include walruses and whales; the fragile ecosystem is slow to change and slow to recover from disruptions or damage; the polar pack ice is thinning.

A Russian nuclear-powered icebreaker carves a path through thick sea ice in the Arctic Ocean.

In addition, other countries touch on the sub-Arctic. The **sub-Arctic** is almost as cold as the Arctic in the winter, but it has warmer summers that allow for a short growing season for plants. These sub-Arctic areas are usually thought by geographers to be part of the Arctic.

EXTENT OF THE ICE

During winter, pack ice covers almost the entire Arctic Ocean. This is frozen seawater, which becomes icy at 28 °F (-2 °C). By March, only the coasts of Norway and Russia (as far as the White Sea) are free of pack ice. Most pack ice is less than 6.5 inches (2 m) thick, and sometimes **icebreakers** are able to plow a way through it.

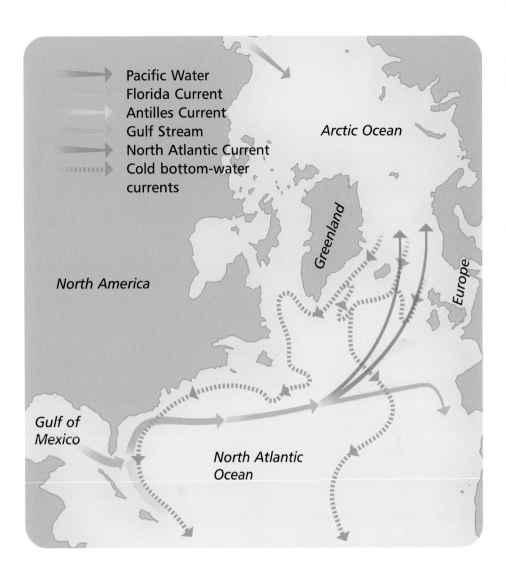

This map shows ocean currents in the Arctic and North Atlantic Oceans. Cold bottom-water flowing out of the Arctic is one of the world's most important ocean currents.

LOCATION FILE

THE BERING STRAIT

Named after the Danish navigator who first explored these northern waters, the Bering Strait is a short stretch of water separating North America from Asia.

During the **Cold War,** the Bering Strait became one of the most heavily defended frontiers in the world. The U.S. and the **USSR** set up military installations and listening posts in an effort to spy on one another and prevent an invasion from the north.

ARCTIC OCEAN CURRENTS

The Arctic's ocean currents have an important effect on the climate of nearby regions. For example, the warm current known as the Gulf Stream is powered partly by a cycle of cold, salty water sinking to the bottom. This is then replaced at the surface by warmer water flowing from the Gulf of Mexico. This warm water gives regions such as northwestern Scotland a warmer climate than they would otherwise experience. In the meantime, cold Arctic bottom-water flows south toward the Antarctic in a powerful current that helps power the movement of ocean waters.

THE ANTARCTIC

Unlike in the Arctic, hidden below the Antarctic ice cap is an actual landmass. Without its ice, Antarctica would be the smallest of the world's seven continents. Including the ice cap, however, the Antarctic covers about 5.6 million square miles (14 million sq km) and is larger than either Europe or Australia.

THE ANTARCTIC ICE CAP

The Antarctic ice cap is an average of roughly 7,216 feet (2,200 m) thick. This means that Antarctica is the highest continent in terms of average elevation, at 7,544 feet (2,300 m) above sea level. Peeking up through the ice cap in places are Antarctica's mountains: the Antarctic Peninsula, pointing up toward Cape Horn; the Trans Antarctic Mountains; and several other, minor ranges.

Some of the ice at the Antarctic's edge has slowly been pushed there from much farther inland, and is thousands of years old.

AN ANCIENT, ICY WORLD

Less than one percent of Antarctica is free of ice and snow, and the region contains 90 percent of the world's total amount of ice. If all this ice melted, the oceans would rise by about 200 to 215 feet (60–65 m). During winter, the sea ice that surrounds Antarctica more than doubles the continent's area.

In places, Antarctica's ice is so old that scientists are able to discover information about the climate of Earth thousands of years ago, by examining the atmospheric traces left behind. They have been able to peer through this icy window on the past and see back 400,000 years (see page 41).

Seeming as though it goes on forever, this is the Ekstrom Ice Shelf, beside the Weddell Sea, in Antarctica. Despite the sunshine, new ice is forming on the ocean's surface.

 FACT FILE

THE ANTARCTIC

* NAME Antarctica
* AREA 5.6 million square miles (14 million sq km)
* POPULATION Around 1,200, excluding tourists
* GOVERNMENT No country governs Antarctica; it is administered by the Antarctic Treaty (see page 37). A number of countries claim territorial rights or maintain bases in Antarctica. They include:

From Europe: France, Britain, Poland, Germany, Ukraine, and Russia

From Asia and Australasia: Australia, New Zealand, South Korea, India, and Japan

From North and South America: Chile, Argentina, U.S., Brazil, and Uruguay

From Africa: South Africa.

This means that countries from each of the world's other six continents could one day claim a slice of the seventh.

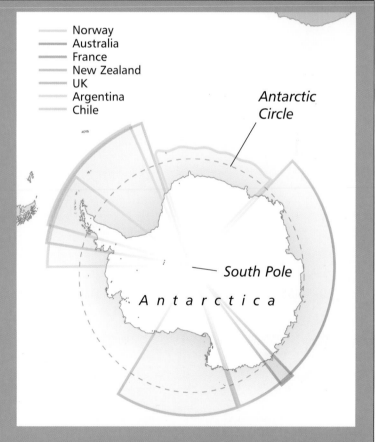

- Norway
- Australia
- France
- New Zealand
- UK
- Argentina
- Chile

Antarctic Circle

— *South Pole*

A n t a r c t i c a

This map shows some of the overlapping claims to Antarctic territory.

A WORLD OF ICE

The features of the polar landscape are unlike anywhere else on Earth. Even though the polar regions contain almost all the world's fresh water, it is frozen solid. So little precipitation falls in the interior of the Antarctic that it can be called a desert. This dry landscape offers little chance of survival for plants, so even where the ground is exposed, nothing grows.

An Inuit hunter races to catch his dog sled. The Inuit successfully adapted to life in the Arctic when they arrived there more than 1,000 years ago.

✴ FACT FILE

Above: Icebergs form when part of an ice shelf (like this one) breaks away. The biggest can be the size of a medium-sized island, even though most of the iceberg is underwater.

ICEBERGS

• From 80 to 90 percent of most icebergs is underwater. But as little as 50 percent and as much as 99 percent can be underwater, depending on the amount of air trapped inside.

• Icebergs are made of fresh water, not seawater.

• One of the biggest icebergs ever seen broke free from the Ross Ice Shelf, in Antarctica, in 1995. Above water, it was 183 miles (295 km) long and 23 miles (37 km) wide—about the size of Connecticut. Below the surface, it was 10 times as big.

THE VINSON MASSIF

The Vinson Massif (above) is the highest point on Antarctica. This means it is on the "tick list" (meaning things to do) of those who want to climb the highest peak on each of the seven continents. This has led to one of the more curious industries in Antarctica—mountain guiding, where specialist climbers escort those with less experience to the top.

Above: **The peak of Mount Vinson, which has now been reached by an increasing number of climbers who are wealthy enough to join an expedition there.**

COMPACTED SNOW

When snow first falls, it is very light, and has a **density** roughly one-third that of solid ice. However, as more snow falls on top of it, the layer underneath begins to be crushed down. Slowly, over decades, it is compacted until it becomes solid ice. This is how the permanent ice cap built up around the South Pole, from snow blown there from the coast by Antarctica's fierce winds.

In the Antarctic, there is a limit to how thick the ice cap can become. Too much pressure from above causes the ice to slowly flow outward. It flows over or around obstacles to the sea. In some places, the ice is warmer under the surface than where it is exposed, and it can even melt, creating ice streams that help lubricate the ice's progress toward the sea.

ICEBERGS AND SEA ICE

When the ice cap meets the sea, it spreads out over the surface of the water for a long way. However, sometimes, huge chunks of ice break away and float off. These are icebergs. Usually they are stuck in place during the winter, but in the summer, when the sea ice melts, giant icebergs are sometimes released that can become a hazard to shipping.

11

TUNDRA AND TAIGA

On the fringes of the Arctic are two zones that surround the northern polar region. They are known as the tundra and taiga. Typically, they have winters that are almost as cold as those of the Arctic itself, but the summers are warmer, allowing a growing season for plants and, in the taiga, trees. The Antarctic's thick ice cannot support tundra or taiga.

THE TUNDRA

Tundra is the name given to the treeless plains that surround the Arctic. The ground thaws in the summer, allowing low-growing plants to put down roots. These include mosses, lichens, grasses, and shrubs. **Migratory** birds and other animals spread into the region, enjoying the brief flush of life summer brings. Others, like the Arctic fox, emerge from their winter coats and adopt a different camouflage from the white they have been wearing during the snowy times. **Meltwater** forms ponds, small lakes, and swamps, which freeze again in the winter. Usually, only the top 1 to 10 feet (30–300 cm) of soil thaws; below that the ground is always frozen. This is called **permafrost**.

The Arctic fox is able to change its coat from winter white to summer colors, which will blend in better with the tundra landscape.

THE TAIGA

South of the tundra lies a zone where the soil thaws more deeply. Here, trees such as dwarf willows, birches, and alders grow. They rarely reach heights of more than 39 feet (12 m), because their roots cannot grow to support a greater height than this. Reindeer moss (so-called because it is eaten by reindeer) covers large areas of ground in a thick, spongy carpet. Farther south again is the taiga: great forests of trees such as cedars, firs, pines, spruce, and birch. This has

The border between the taiga forests of the Denali National Park, Alaska, and the tundra that lies farther north.

become a major resource for loggers. Although the winter lasts for seven or eight months, the growing season has long hours of daylight in which plants can **photosynthesize**. There is also reliable rainfall, so a lot of growth can be packed into a short summer.

LOCATION FILE

THULE, GREENLAND

One major tundra region is Thule, in north-western Greenland. Lying just north of the Arctic Circle, Thule is the site of a U.S. airbase, so it provides many Americans with their first experience of Arctic living. It is named after "Ultima Thule," a place described roughly 2,000 years ago by a Greek writer named Pytheas. "Ultima Thule" was the most northern land known—Pytheas said that the days and nights lasted six months each, and the ice was so thick that it could not be rowed through.

CLIMATE

T he climate of the polar regions varies depending on how near to the pole one is. But all regions would seem extremely cold during the winter to anyone who had never visited them before. They are also extremely dry: the Antarctic interior gets so little rain that it is technically a desert, and the Arctic is also a parched land.

EXTREMES OF COLD

Most household freezers run at about -4 °F (-20 °C). In the Arctic, the average winter temperature is about -29 °F (-34 °C). The coldest weather of all is found in north-eastern Siberia, where a lowest-ever temperature of -92 °F (-69 °C) was once recorded. Temperatures in Antarctica regularly fall even lower.

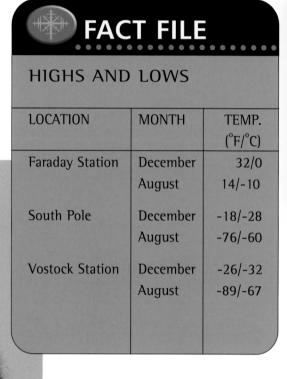

FACT FILE

HIGHS AND LOWS

LOCATION	MONTH	TEMP. (°F/°C)
Faraday Station	December	32/0
	August	14/-10
South Pole	December	-18/-28
	August	-76/-60
Vostock Station	December	-26/-32
	August	-89/-67

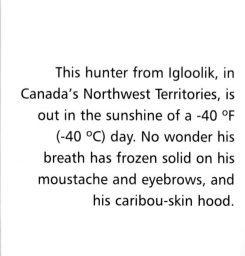

This hunter from Igloolik, in Canada's Northwest Territories, is out in the sunshine of a -40 °F (-40 °C) day. No wonder his breath has frozen solid on his moustache and eyebrows, and his caribou-skin hood.

Nearer to the coast, both polar regions have warmer climates. In the Antarctic summertime, January inland temperatures reach only about 5 ºF (-15 ºC). At the coasts, they may reach 32 ºF (0 ºC). Some northern islands even manage 50 ºF (10 ºC)—not exactly hot, but not so cold that a person's hand would freeze to any metal it touches, as it would in winter!

The Arctic climate also changes depending on location. Average summer temperatures near the Atlantic and Pacific Oceans are 45 ºF (7 ºC). However, inland parts of Siberia and North America are even warmer in the summer, with highs of 90 ºF (32 ºC) or more.

DRY REGIONS

Rainfall in the Arctic averages between 6 and 10 inches (15–25 cm) a year, including melted snow. This may seem low, but compared with the Antarctic, it's a lot. The interior **plateau** of Antarctica averages just two inches (5 cm) of snow a year. Even on the coast, an average of just 23 inches (60 cm) of snow falls.

Wearing plenty of layers of clothes is essential in cold weather. Air trapped between the layers warms up, keeping a person warmer than a single layer might.

LOCATION FILE

THE COLDEST PLACE ON EARTH
• The coldest average temperature was recorded at Plateau Station, Antarctica, with an average of -71 ºF (-57 ºC).
• The coldest temperature ever recorded on Earth was at Vostok Station, Antarctica. The temperature gauge there fell to -128 ºF (-89 ºC), on July 21, 1983.

WEATHER

The polar regions experience some of the most violent weather conditions on Earth. Extremely powerful winds batter the landscape, especially in winter. In coastal regions, especially in the sub-Arctic, heavy snow can trap people indoors for days on end. Parts of the Arctic even suffer from extreme heat—in the middle of summer, the temperature can rise above 90 °F (32 °C)!

POLAR WINDS

Both polar regions experience very high wind speeds. These add a **wind chill** factor to the temperature, whereby the force of the wind takes heat away from living things more quickly than if there were no wind. In the Antarctic winter, **katabatic winds** flow down from the continent's interior toward the coast as cold air is drawn to the warmer regions near the ocean.

Adult emperor penguins have surrounded a group of their chicks as a way of offering them some shelter from a blizzard.

FACT FILE

A WEIGHT OF ICE

• Antarctica is pushed into the planet by the weight of the ice that covers it. If all the ice were removed, the continent would spring up by about 1,640 feet (500 m)—but very slowly. It would grow an average of about two inches (5 cm) a year.

• Scotland and Scandinavia, also buried under an ice sheet long ago, are both still rebounding. The "fastest" place is in the northern Baltic—where the growth is about .2 inches (5 mm) a year.

A sudden winter storm hits the community of Savissivick, in northwestern Greenland.

STORMS

In the Arctic winter, storms develop mainly in two areas where the air temperature is almost always low. The first is the Aleutian low, which extends from eastern Siberia to the Gulf of Alaska. The second is the Icelandic low, which covers central Canada, the Arctic Ocean, and part of the northern Atlantic and northern Europe. Weather stations in Alaska warn of storms approaching northern North America, while forecasters in Greenland and Iceland help to predict storms arriving in Europe.

To the north of the Antarctic lies a belt of strong westerly winds. These drive both weather and the ocean currents, at a latitude known as the "Roaring Forties." Ocean-racing yachts often try to use the Roaring Forties to gain speed. But these are dangerous waters, and many sailors have lost their lives here through the years.

Occasionally, storm systems develop in the Roaring Forties and spin down toward Antarctica. They bring strong winds and heavy snow to the coasts, but few storms ever reach the high interior plateau.

 LOCATION FILE

CAPE DENISON, ADÉLIE LAND COAST, ANTARCTICA
• On the steep coastal slopes of Cape Denison, the Antarctic's katabatic winds accelerate to speeds of more than 434 miles (700 km) per hour.
• In 1912-13, an expedition led by Sir Douglas Mawson recorded a world-record sustained wind speed of 62 feet (19 m) per second.
• On all but one of 203 days, the Mawson expedition experienced gale-force winds.

POLAR OCEANS

Most scientists place the northern limit of the Antarctic Ocean between 40° and 60° south latitude, though its boundaries are not universally agreed. The Arctic Ocean is usually said to be made up of most of the waters that lie north of the Arctic Circle. Groups of islands divide the ocean into seven seas (see fact file on page 19).

FROZEN SURFACES

In the winter, large areas of both polar oceans are frozen over. About 70 percent of the Arctic Ocean is covered in ice throughout the year. This ice circulates slowly in a clockwise direction, driven by the easterly airflow of the region and its ocean currents. The Antarctic Ocean develops ice along the coastline of Antarctica. In the summer, the ice occupies more than one million square miles (2.5 million sq km); in the winter, it can spread to more than eight million (20.5 million).

Very few Arctic ports stay open year-round, because sea ice freezes so hard and deep that ships cannot escape. They have to sit ice-bound in the harbor, waiting for the spring thaw.

LOCATION FILE

DRAKE PASSAGE

The Antarctic Ocean's narrowest point is the 620-foot (1,000 km) gap between Antarctica and Tierra del Fuego, the southern tip of South America. Here, wind-driven currents push a tremendous amount of water through the Drake Passage—enough to equal roughly 5,000 times the flow of the Amazon River.

OCEAN CURRENTS

Near to Antarctica, the winds flow in an easterly direction, causing the ocean current around the continent to flow east as well. Farther north, strong westerly winds create a west-flowing current. The place where these two currents rub against one another is known as the Antarctic Divergence. Farther north still, the Antarctic Convergence marks the place where warmer waters meet the cold polar sea.

More than half the water that flows into the Arctic Ocean comes from the North Atlantic Current, flowing between Iceland and Norway. Most of the rest flows north from the Pacific, through the Bering Strait. Water leaves the ocean in the East Greenland Current and through a current that flows through the islands of the Canadian Arctic. Bottom-water moving south from the Arctic is known as the Great Conveyor, which finally joins the Circumpolar Current in the Antarctic.

RESOURCES

Although they appear to be barren lands covered by snow for much of each year, the polar regions are rich in resources. Whether these should be exploited is a constant source of conflict. The Antarctic is protected by an international treaty that prevents any commercial activity. The Arctic has no treaty, and its resources have been plundered by people from the south for hundreds of years.

WHALE HO!

One of the first Arctic resources to be exploited was whales. In the 1600s, whaling became a major industry in Europe, and demand for **whale oil**, **spermaceti**, and **baleen** became unquenchable. Whale products were used for lamp oil at a time when lamps were almost the only source of light, as well as in clothing manufacture and many other processes. By the 1700s, whalers had spread their activities throughout the Arctic. It was the crew of a whaling ship that first set foot on the continent of Antarctica. So many whales were killed that in the early 1700s, the U.S. whaling fleet alone was taking about 10,000 a year. Whale numbers dropped so low that today whales are protected, and may be hunted only for scientific purposes.

The whaling ship *Essex* being attacked and sunk by a giant male sperm whale, an incident that inspired the novel *Moby Dick*. Whales rarely came out of encounters with whaling ships on the winning side, however, and hundreds of thousands were hunted during the 19th and 20th centuries.

FISHING

Some of the world's richest fishing grounds lie along the edges of polar regions, off the coasts of Greenland and Iceland. In the Antarctic, the seas are rich in krill, small shrimp-like creatures that in large numbers can turn the ocean red by their color. The krill attract many kinds of fish, which in turn attract fishing vessels to the region's seas.

WEALTH UNDER THE GROUND

The Antarctic continent has various minerals, including gold. These minerals occur in small amounts, however, and because of the difficult climate, it would probably not be worthwhile to extract them.

The lands that fringe the Arctic Ocean are home to a variety of minerals, most of which are worth mining. Oil and natural gas are also found in valuable quantities. Greenland is the site of the world's only large deposit of cryolite, which is used in making aluminum and glass.

FORESTS

The trees of the taiga can reach up to 82 feet (25 m) in height. The forests that fringe the polar lands have been logged for centuries, but in the last 100 years they have begun to disappear at a higher rate than ever before. In parts of eastern North America, for example, less than two percent of the original forest remains.

EARLY HISTORY

Thousands of years ago, people in search of new lands began to use a land bridge formed by the dry Bering Strait (which has now disappeared beneath the ocean) to cross from Asia to North America. These early travelers were just passing through the polar regions, however. It was only the last group of emigrants from Asia who stayed put in the Arctic. Today their descendants are known as the Inuit, Aleut, and Yuit peoples.

LIVING AS A GROUP

Life in the harsh conditions of the Arctic was extremely tough. Everyone was expected to help with the day-to-day activities that made life possible. Behavior that threatened the group could result in **banishment**. Since individuals cannot survive alone in the Arctic, banishment was nearly always a death sentence.

When food was plentiful, Inuit people lived in groups that could include several hundred members. For example, in the spring and autumn in Alaska, the caribou migrated, and large groups gathered at the best hunting grounds. When food was less plentiful, people split into smaller groups that would find it easier to feed themselves.

FOOD AND CLOTHING

With few plants available to eat, people had to survive mainly by hunting. Most groups lived near the sea, where they caught whales and seals, as well as Arctic char, salmon, and other fish. On land, they hunted caribou, as well as smaller animals such as hares and foxes.

The Inuit dressed in clothes made of animal skins: caribou was considered best (as the animal was easiest to catch, and its large hide was both warm and hard-wearing), followed by sealskin, fox, polar bear, and other skins. People wore a hooded jacket called a parka, trousers, boots, and mittens, as well as other layers on the inside for warmth.

The 500-year-old face of a mummified Inuit child, found with seven other mummies in Greenland in 1972.

When this photo was taken in 1910, the way of life of northern people had begun to change. Even so, these women could not have imagined that their grandchildren would one day be using snowmobiles to get around.

TRANSPORTATION AND SHELTER

In the summer, most people walked on land and traveled by boat on water. They spent most of their time living in tents.

In the winter, people traveled the ice using dog sleds. For shelter, they dug down into the ground, then lined the hole with stones. Wood or whalebone made the roof, which was covered in earth. Often the entrance to this kind of house was underground so that the warm air inside could not rise into the outside air and escape.

FACT FILE

ANIMAL USES

Arctic peoples used every possible part of the animals they caught. Some of the uses they found for parts of the animals are quite surprising:

• People often wore goggles to protect their eyes from the glare of the sun on the snow. These could be made of bone or **walrus ivory**. Goggles had small holes or slits to look through.

• Seal or caribou skins were used to cover the tents people usually lived in during the summer.

• **Kayaks** and **umiaks** were made of wooden frameworks covered in sealskin.

POLAR EXPLORATION

Explorers who aimed to reach the actual sites of the North and South Poles had to be able to deal with the extreme cold, high winds, and snowstorms that are common in the polar regions. The North Pole, more accessible from inhabited areas, was reached first, in 1909. Then in 1911, the South Pole was reached.

EARLY ARCTIC EXPLORERS

The first people to explore the Arctic regions were migrants from Asia, who are now known as the Inuit, Aleut, and Yuit people (see pages 22 and 23). The first Europeans interested in Arctic exploration were looking for a way to reach Asia by traveling through the icy northern seas. This route was known as the **Northwest Passage**, and many men died trying to discover if it really existed.

FACT FILE

POLAR MILESTONES
- 1570s Martin Frobisher journeys into Arctic regions searching for the Northwest Passage.
- 1773 James Cook crosses the Antarctic Circle while searching for Antarctica.
- 1820 Antarctica is seen for the first time.
- 1839–43 James Ross is the first to journey beyond the pack ice surrounding Antarctica.
- 1845 Sir John Franklin's expedition disappears while searching for a sea route around northern North America.
- 1901–02 Robert Scott leads the first inland exploration of Antarctica.
- 1909 Robert Peary reaches the North Pole.
- 1911 Roald Amundsen reaches the South Pole.

THE NORTH POLE IS REACHED

In the late 1800s, explorers began to visit the Arctic hoping to become the first to reach the Pole. American Robert E. Peary is said to have led the expedition that got there first, on April 6, 1909. He traveled to the Pole with Matthew Henson and four Inuit men on dog sleds.

Admiral Robert E. Peary, an American, is credited with leading the first successful expedition to the North Pole.

Four members of Scott's team drag supplies from their ship.

ANTARCTIC EXPLORATION

The first people to sight Antarctica almost certainly set eyes on it in 1820. Three sailors—British and Russian navy officers and an American sealer—separately reached points where the continent was visible. It wasn't until 1895 that a Norwegian named Henryk Johan Bull and his crew of whalers actually set foot on Antarctica.

RACE TO THE SOUTH POLE

By the early 1900s, several explorers were aiming to be the first to journey to the South Pole. By 1911, it had become a race between two teams, one led by Roald Amundsen of Norway, and the other by Robert Scott of Great Britain. Scott's expedition aimed to use ponies and motor sleds, but these became bogged down in the snow. The men were forced to drag much of their gear themselves.

Amundsen, by contrast, was using Inuit techniques to make better progress. He and his four assistants traveled by ski, reaching the Pole on December 14, 1911, and returning to their base camp safely. Scott reached the Pole on January 17, 1912. He and his team of four men died during the attempt to return home.

One of Amundsen's men with his team of six fast-moving sled dogs.

FACT FILE

LEARNING FROM THE INUIT

The expeditions that reached the Poles first made use of Inuit techniques for travel and survival:

• Dog teams hauled equipment, making faster progress than the men could dragging the gear themselves.

• When killed and eaten, the dogs provided emergency food supplies.

• The explorers journeyed on skis, and wore relatively light, warm furs to survive the freezing temperatures.

POLAR PEOPLES

The biting cold and extreme weather of the actual Poles ought to mean that no one lives there. But in fact, the U.S. has maintained an international scientific research base at the South Pole since 1956. No one lives at the North Pole, but native people and a few others do live near enough to be called inhabitants of the Arctic, rather than sub-Arctic.

ANTARCTIC RESEARCH STATIONS

The only people living on the Antarctic continent are those based at scientific research stations. The most amazing of these is America's Amundsen-Scott South Pole Station, which is actually at the Pole. But many other countries maintain bases in Antarctica (see page 9), too. The scientists and others who live in these are cocooned from the weather in modern facilities, but nonetheless, they risk being cut off from civilization for long periods. When conditions allow, they leave the stations to go on field trips.

Modern times: a Nunavut hunter in a traditional parka uses a satellite phone.

FACT FILE

ALASKA PERMANENT FUND

The Alaska Permanent Fund (APF) is a savings account that belongs to all the people in Alaska. The money in it comes from taxes on mineral developments, including oil.

• Alaska's mineral resources brought the state so much income that in 1980 it abolished individual **income tax**.

• Each year, 50 percent of the earnings of the APF are divided equally among Alaska's residents.

These houses are in the Inuit territory of Nunavut, Canada. The territory occupies a large part of the Canadian Arctic.

NATIVE PEOPLES

In the Arctic, native peoples such as the Inuit still live in the territories they have occupied for hundreds of years. Their way of life has changed: very few still live on the land as their ancestors did. Instead of tents in the summer and dug-in houses in the winter, they live in prefabricated homes. These are shipped ready-made from farther south and then assembled into communities. Hunters are likely to go out onto the ice using a snowmobile and wearing cold-weather gear filled with down (see page 35), rather than a dog sled and sealskin parka.

The change from traditional lifestyles has brought problems for some native people. In particular, alcoholism has affected many communities. On the other hand, they now have access to healthcare and education opportunities that didn't exist in the past.

OIL AND INDUSTRY

Relatively new arrivals in the Arctic have been brought there by modern industry. Alaska and Siberia, for example, are both crossed by pipelines hundreds of miles long. These were built to carry oil from the oil wells of the far north to distribution centers farther to the south. People from the south are drawn to the Arctic lands to work on these and other modern industrial developments.

(see page 35)

LOCATION FILE

NUNAVUT

Nunavut (shaded deep blue on the map below) is the name of a region of northern Canada that is now a homeland for Inuit people. They are able to exercise **self-government** there, while remaining part of the Canadian nation.

• Nunavut came into being in 1999; its capital is Iqaluit.
• It makes up roughly one-fifth of Canada's total area.
• Nunavut means "Our Land" in an Inuit language.

SUB-ARCTIC PEOPLES

A round the European and Asian fringes of the Arctic live peoples who herd reindeer. The herds move north in the summer. Then in the winter, they head back south, where they spend the cold months in warmer conditions. On the North American fringes of the Arctic, small bands of Native Americans once lived by hunting and gathering food. Unfortunately, sub-Arctic peoples have seen their traditional ways of life slowly disappear.

A HERDING EXISTENCE

Groups such as the Nenets, from Siberia, and the Saami, from northern Europe, traditionally lived by herding reindeer. In the winter, they headed north to allow the reindeer to **graze** on the mosses and lichens that had been uncovered in the thaw. As the weather turned wintry again, they would pack up their camps and head south, to find warmer pastures.

Twice each year, the reindeer herders of the sub-Arctic make the long journey with their herds to reach new pastures.

FACT FILE

THREATS TO SUB-ARCTIC PEOPLES

There are several key threats to the traditional lifestyles of sub-Arctic peoples:
• Pollution from the former USSR has poisoned the reindeer meat, making it dangerous to eat in some regions.
• Animal rights campaigners have made it impossible to sell the furs of the animals the native people hunt or herd.
• Commercial activities, such as logging, oil and gas extraction, or hydroelectric power schemes, have made land impossible to use.

AN EXTRACT FROM THE WORK OF YEREMI AIPIN, A KHANT WRITER FROM SIBERIA

"The loggers even cut down the trees on the tribal cemetery, thus ruining the final resting place. In all his 76 years, my father had not once plucked a fir needle or a leaf, not a blade of grass unnecessarily on his land, the land of his ancestors.

'What do you want, old man?' I ask my father. 'Can I help you?'

'I don't want anything,' he says after a long silence. 'Only my land. Give me back my land where I can graze my reindeer, hunt game, and catch fish. Give me my land where my deer are not attacked by stray dogs and poachers, where the rivers and lakes have no oil slicks—just a patch of my own land.'

What can I say in reply?"

Below: A village in Chukotka, Siberia. Native peoples in this region found life very difficult under Russia's old communist government, and many still struggle to live their traditional lifestyle.

CHANGING LIFESTYLES

Today, few sub-Arctic peoples live a traditional lifestyle. Only about 10 percent of Saami people, for example, are still **nomadic** reindeer herders. Most no longer live as they once did. Often their land has been taken for other uses, or ruined by pollution. This loss of their lifestyle, often without anything to replace it, has a bad effect on people. Some fall into despair, and become dependent on alcohol or drugs.

NON-NATIVE PEOPLES

More non-native people also live on the fringes of the Arctic than farther north. Oil workers, forestry workers, fishermen, educators, and public officials all live in the established communities.

SURVIVAL SKILLS

L ife in the polar regions has always been a struggle against the harsh environment. The people of the Arctic developed their clothes and homes in response to the conditions, and usually live safely. But sometimes things go wrong. A hunter may be trapped on the ice by a sudden storm, or become lost in unfamiliar territory. In these situations, specialist skills are needed to survive.

SHELTER

Shelter is crucial to anyone caught out in a frozen environment, especially at night. There are various types of snow shelters: the favorite of Inuit people is the **igloo**. Some people think these are what Inuit used to live in, but the Inuit have really only ever used them as they do now, for temporary overnight shelter. Nenets reindeer herders carry a tent and stove with them as overnight shelter. A third shelter option in the Arctic is to make a snow cave in a snowy slope.

KEEPING WARM

Unless one has some way of starting a fire, keeping warm in the polar regions in an emergency will probably depend on shelter and clothing. Once a shelter has been arranged, it is very important for a person to keep his or her **extremities**, especially the head, warm, as a lot of body heat is lost through them. Huddling up close to another person reduces the amount of body heat a single body would lose on its own. It is also important for a person to wear all the clothes he or she has, instead of waiting to add another layer. Lying on the ground or snow should be avoided. A backpack, leaves, branches, or almost anything will insulate a body from the cold ground, even if only a little.

FACT FILE

SURVIVAL KIT

A polar survival kit might include the following:
- Ice saw, for cutting blocks of ice to make shelter.
- Compass, to avoid walking in circles across the snowy landscape.
- Waterproof matches.
- Plastic survival bag, to crawl inside and retain heat/keep dry.
- Mini solid-fuel stove with fuel.
- Flares.

An Inuit hunter lights his stove inside his newly built igloo.

Field training for Antarctic researchers, teaching them how to deal with one of the deadliest environments on Earth.

 **FACT FILE**

RULES FOR AN EMERGENCY SHELTER IN VERY COLD CLIMATES

- If the entrance is lower than the living space, it won't let heat out.
- Make sure the entrance faces away from the wind.
- Ventilate the space with two air holes to avoid suffocation.
- Small shelters are easier to keep warm.
- Keep a digging tool inside, so you can dig yourself out if snowed in.
- Mark the shelter with a flag—it will make the shelter easier to find in the snow.

Top (interior view) and middle (exterior view): For short stays only—a simple dug-out shelter with an ice-block roof and a brushwood floor for insulation.

Bottom: A longer-stay shelter—to trap heat, this shelter has a low-down door, brushwood insulation, and a brushwood cover.

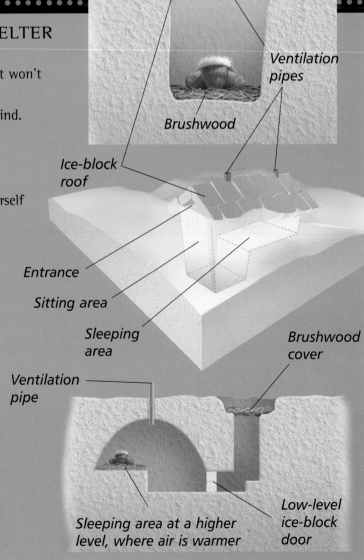

Ventilation pipes

Brushwood

Ice-block roof

Entrance

Sitting area

Sleeping area

Ventilation pipe

Brushwood cover

Sleeping area at a higher level, where air is warmer

Low-level ice-block door

31

POLAR LAND ANIMALS

Penguins and seals visit the coastal areas of Antarctica at times during the year, but no large land-based creatures can survive the climate permanently. The Arctic is a richer environment: because it touches on the surrounding lands, animals have the opportunity to escape the most severe weather.

SPECIAL ADAPTATIONS

Animals that live in the polar regions have to be specially adapted to the extreme conditions. In particular, they need a thick coat to help them survive the icy winds and low temperatures. Arctic hares and foxes have short ears and tails, to stop them from losing too much body heat. In the worst of the cold weather, polar animals have a choice: they can either hide from the weather, or travel to warmer lands to escape it.

HIBERNATING FOR THE WINTER

One way to escape the winter storms and cold is to go to sleep until spring, living off the fat the body has stored during the summer. Polar bears, for example, go into a kind of **hibernation** in a

Caribou, a kind of reindeer, live throughout much of the sub-Arctic. They provide native peoples with meat and skins to make into clothing.

POLAR BEARS

• There are an estimated 25,000 polar bears in the Arctic. About 15,000 of them live in Canada.

• In 1973, Greenland, Norway, Canada, the U.S., and the USSR signed the International Agreement for the Conservation of Polar Bears, in an effort to protect the bears from extinction.

• Nonetheless, polar bears are still threatened by pollution, poaching, hunting, and a shorter hunting season caused by the early springtime melting of the ice in Hudson Bay.

One of the Arctic's most recognizable animals—a polar bear, with her cub.

cave or snowhole for the winter, before emerging feeling very hungry in the springtime. Polar bear cubs are usually born just before their mother emerges from her hibernation place, so the first weather they see is the Arctic spring.

ESCAPING THE COLD

Some animals head south of the true Arctic for the winter. Herds of caribou, for example, spend the warmer summer months grazing on the tundra. During the winter, as the temperatures on the tundra get colder, they head south. The winter can be spent in the shelter of the evergreen taiga forests, where the temperatures are higher, and there is more protection from the wind.

AN ANTARCTIC GIANT

The largest land animal in Antarctica is an insect less than .5 inches (1.3 cm) long. It is a wingless midge (if it had wings, the wind would blow it away) that hops on its tail to get around, and usually lives near penguin colonies.

POLAR SEA CREATURES

During the feeding season in Antarctica, a full-grown blue whale eats about 40 million krill (shrimp-like creatures) a day. That's enough to feed a human for four years! Yet the seas are so rich that there are enough krill to support this feeding.

PLANKTON

One of the most important parts of the polar ocean **food chain** is plankton, tiny creatures that thrive in the polar seas. Plantlike organisms among the plankton are called phytoplankton, while the animal organisms are called zooplankton. Krill, for example, are a type of zooplankton.

The plankton is eaten by other sea creatures, from small fish (which are then eaten by bigger fish) to the world's largest animal, the blue whale.

The male Atlantic walrus can grow to almost 13 feet (4 m) long and weigh 3,100 pounds (1,400 kg). Its tusks can reach three feet (1 m) in length.

AQUATIC ANIMALS

Animals such as whales, dolphins, and fish are fully aquatic—they spend all their time in the sea. In the past, these animals have provided a rich resource. Cod in particular has been a popular catch around the Arctic for hundreds of years. There is even evidence that Basque cod fishermen reached North America long before Columbus— but kept it secret because of the rich cod-fishing grounds off the coast! In Antarctica, the main commercial fish is the Patagonian toothfish.

AMPHIBIOUS ANIMALS

Some animals—penguins, seals, and walruses, for example—hunt for food in the sea but rest on land. This "wet n' dry" lifestyle is called amphibious. The amphibious animals eat fish and shellfish, and are in turn hunted by one of the world's most fearsome predators, the killer whale.

THE GRAND BANKS

The Grand Banks is a fishing ground off the coast of Newfoundland. Plankton thrive in the shallow waters, attracting fish, including cod, in large numbers. The cod provide a good example of what can happen when a polar resource is overused.

Today, the cod have been **over-fished**. The fish caught in the northern Atlantic are far smaller than those of 200 years ago, which were the size of a full-grown man. Cod numbers have probably reached a point where they cannot recover (see pages 36 and 37).

Cod drying in the Newfoundland sun.

POLAR BIRDS

• The old squaw duck, willow ptarmigans, and eider ducks are the most common Arctic birds.
• The eider duck's soft breast feathers are especially prized for use in duvets, sleeping bags, and coats, as they trap air for warmth but are extremely light.
• Penguins (left) are the Antarctic's most common birds. Their coat of feathers is waterproof, and they have a thick layer of fat for insulation against the cold.

A colony of penguins in Antarctica.

COMMERCIAL EXPLOITATIO

The polar regions are unique environments that have built up over hundreds of thousands of years. They can easily be changed by pollution, mineral extraction, farming of their natural resources (such as seals or whales), and settlement by humans. Once they are damaged, it is uncertain when, or even whether, they will recover.

WHALING AND FISHING

Fishing and whaling provide good examples of how the polar environment can be changed by human actions. During the 18th and 19th centuries, the world's whales were hunted by large fleets of ships. Some species were brought to the brink of extinction.

During the 20th century, cod was fished to such high levels that it seems unlikely ever to recover. Breeding stocks are now so low that the cod may have lost their place on the food chain. They would now find it impossible to increase their numbers, because their food resources are being eaten by other species.

This gas-drilling rig is located in Siberia. Oil and gas are among the Arctic's richest resources.

THE ARCTIC NATIONAL WILDLIFE RESERVE

In 2002, this reserve in northeastern Alaska was threatened with being opened to oil drilling.

• President Bush claimed that the Reserve could be part of a long-term answer to America's "energy crisis."

• Opponents said that the drilling and pipelines would have a serious effect on the wildlife within the reserve, especially caribou and musk oxen, whose migration routes would be interrupted.

• The U.S. Geological Survey had said in 1998 that only between 3.2 and 5.2 billion barrels of oil were recoverable from the reserve—a six-month supply for the U.S.

On April 18, 2002, the U.S. Senate voted against allowing oilmen into the Arctic National Wildlife Reserve.

Below: **Caribou swim large distances on their migration routes. Their overland routes would be cut if oil drilling starts in the Arctic National Wildlife Reserve.**

ARCTIC COMMERCIAL ACTIVITY

In the Arctic, big businesses are keen to make money by extracting the region's minerals. There is already oil drilling, gas extraction, and mining in the Arctic. Even places that are supposed to be protected, such as wildlife reserves, are sometimes not safe.

THE ANTARCTIC TREATY

The Antarctic is "ruled" through the Antarctic Treaty, which was signed by 12 countries in 1961. Since then, 32 others have joined, and the Treaty represents 80 percent of the world's people. It says that the Antarctic is a natural reserve, devoted to peace and scientific research.

POLLUTION

Because the polar regions have little industry of their own and a very low population density, one might think that they would not suffer from pollution. In fact, pollution reaches polar seas on ocean currents, and polar lands through the air. This is especially true of the Arctic, which lies nearer to major industrial nations.

OIL POLLUTION

In both Alaska and Siberia, long oil pipelines carry oil from the oil fields to ice-free tanker ports. Leaks in the pipelines can spread crude oil over a large area very quickly. This affects the animals and people who live there, and can **contaminate** the soil for many years.

Oil also pollutes the waters of the polar regions. In 1989, the oil tanker *Exxon Valdez* ran aground in Prince William Sound, Alaska, spilling nearly 13 million gallons (50 million l) of oil, which was still affecting local wildlife years later.

RADIOACTIVITY

In Siberia, reindeer pastures have been affected by fallout (radioactive pollution) from nuclear testing done during the Cold War (see page 7). Then, in 1986, an accident at the Chernobyl nuclear power plant in the Ukraine spread radioactive pollution right across northern Europe and into the Arctic. The reindeer pastures were contaminated, making it impossible for many herders to sell reindeer meat. Some were forced away from their traditional lifestyles.

Part of the huge clean-up operation after the *Exxon Valdez* oil spill in 1989.

POLLUTION AND THE FOOD CHAIN

Once some pollutants (**organochlorines**, for example) reach the polar regions in the air or on ocean currents, they **concentrate** on their way up the food chain. For example, imagine 100 small fish have one unit of pollutant inside them. These are eaten by a larger fish, which then has 100 units of pollutant. Then a seal eats 100 of the larger fish, meaning it has 10,000 units of pollutant. If a polar bear manages to eat several seals, it will quickly amass very high levels of pollutant.

Some other, more toxic pollutants (such as **organophosphates**) do not concentrate in the same way.

FACT FILE

POLLUTED POLAR BEARS
• Scientists are worried that levels of **PCBs** among polar bears on Norway's Svalbard Islands are far higher than in North America. Norwegian polar bears have PCB levels that can be more than 2.5 times as high as their American cousins.
• PCB levels among polar bears in parts of Canada are also excessive.
• In Russia, the polar bear population is said to have PCB levels 17 times as high as in North America.

PEOPLE FILE

THE SAAMI
The Saami live in northern Norway, Sweden, Finland, and Russia.
• In 1986, the Chernobyl nuclear disaster spread radioactive pollution across Saami pastures. Unable to sell or eat their reindeer meat, many Saami left their traditional way of life.
• Even worse, it emerged later that the level of contamination was very low, which meant that the ban was probably a panic reaction that did more harm than good.

Signs warn that this forest near Chernobyl, Ukraine, is dangerous because of radioactivity.

GLOBAL WARMING

The Antarctic ice cap is the largest body of fresh water in the world, about 70 percent of the world's total. If this ice were to melt, sea levels would rise. The effects of this could be catastrophic. Fortunately, this is not predicted to happen for thousands of years, if ever: the world's average temperature is rising by about one degree per century.

Environmental campaigners say that the reason for temperature rises is that the world produces too many greenhouse gases, especially carbon dioxide. These gases help trap heat in the atmosphere, leading to a rise in temperature known as global warming (see diagram right).

SEA LEVEL RISES

The Antarctic ice cap alone contains enough water to raise sea levels by 200 feet (60 m). Environmentalists fear that if sea levels rose by even a fraction of this, it would cause huge problems. Major cities such as New York and Los Angeles would be threatened by flooding. Coastal plains would be underwater. The world's growing population would be squeezed into an ever-smaller space.

TEMPERATURE RISE AND THE ICE CAPS

So far, the rises in temperature seem to be having little effect on the ice caps. The West Antarctic Ice Sheet has been losing mass for several thousand years—since long before concerns about global temperature rises—and the rate of loss remains constant. The East Antarctic Ice Sheet is stable and likely to remain so: melting it would require a fairly substantial temperature rise. The Greenland Ice Sheet is losing mass in some places, but the effect is minimal.

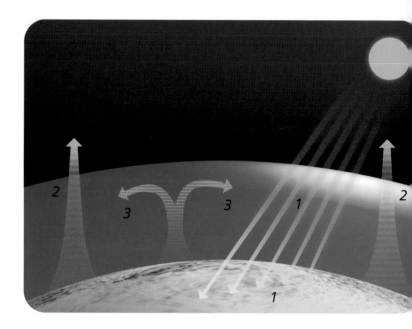

The Greenhouse Effect: the name given to the process where too much of the sun's heat is trapped in Earth's atmosphere, leading to global warming. Heat from the sun warms the atmosphere and the land (1). Some heat escapes (2), but more heat is absorbed by the atmosphere (3), adding to the overall temperature.

FACT FILE

RISES IN SEA LEVEL

• Arctic sea ice has thinned by 40 percent in the past three decades, and its area has possibly shrunk by as much as 10 to 15 percent.

• The global average sea level has risen by four to eight inches (10–20 cm) over the past 100 years. It is expected to rise by another 4 to 30 inches (10–77 cm) by 2100.

CHANGES IN TEMPERATURE

Scientists have examined cores of ice from Greenland and Antarctica to discover whether changes in carbon dioxide levels cause temperature changes:

• The ancient ice provides a record of the atmosphere for the past 160,000 years. During those years, the climate warmed and cooled several times.

• Researchers analyzed the gases that were trapped in the ice when it formed.

• During cooler periods, the atmosphere contained about 30 percent less carbon dioxide than in warmer periods. (It is likely that the change in carbon dioxide concentration was a consequence of climate change, not its cause. The carbon dioxide level rose some centuries after the temperature rose.)

Warmer air has caused this ice in Antarctica to melt into a layered pattern. The honeycombing in the ice in the background is also caused by temperature rise.

THE KYOTO PROTOCOL

In 1997, 38 of the world's nations signed the Kyoto Protocol to try to cut their greenhouse gas emissions. Unfortunately, they have been largely unsuccessful. The U.S., the world's biggest polluter, has backed out of the Protocol, and other nations are lukewarm about supporting it. The main factor is the economic cost. It is also feared that people accustomed to car ownership and other luxuries of modern life will react badly to having some of these reduced.

In light of this, sea levels seem likely to rise over the coming decades. The best estimate is for a rise of 1.6 feet (0.49 m) between 1990 and 2100. This is unlikely to have drastic global consequences, but it could have a serious effect on some low-lying coastal regions.

41

POLAR TOURISM

Despite their inhospitable nature, the polar regions are attracting increasing numbers of tourists. People come to see the wildlife, experience the unique environment, see the Northern or Southern Lights, or go hunting. Antarctica is even home to a very small mountaineering industry!

LIFESTYLE TOURISM

Some people come to the polar lands, usually the Arctic, to get a taste of the lifestyle of its native peoples. They can ride a dog sled, be guided on the ice by Inuit guides, go **ice fishing**—even learn to build an igloo. These tourists tend to bring money to the local economy, because local people provide them with a service for which they are paid.

WILDLIFE TOURS

Other tourists come to see the polar wildlife. For example, in Churchill, Canada, it's possible to see polar bears out on the ice. Some bears even wander into town, where they can be watched from the safety of a taxi or from indoors. Other polar settlements specialize in whale-watching visits or trips to see sea lions. Again, this type of tourism brings money to the local economy.

CRUISING

Cruising—being transported from place to place on a **self-contained** luxury boat—is increasingly popular in polar waters. Passengers get to see icebergs and the ice shelf up close, as well as the animals that live there. They suffer little of the discomfort associated with the polar seas, as they can stay warm in their cabins and eat food like that found in any hotel around the world.

An Inuit park warden on Ellesmere Island, Canada, shows tourists how an old stone fox trap worked.

These tourists in the Antarctic have abandoned their ship for smaller boats so that they can get a closer look at a seal.

TEN PRINCIPLES FOR ARCTIC TOURISM

These ground rules come from WWF, the global environment network:

1. Make tourism and conservation compatible.
2. Support the preservation of wilderness and **biodiversity**.
3. Use natural resources in a sustainable way.
4. Minimize consumption, waste, and pollution.
5. Respect local cultures.
6. Respect historic and scientific sites.
7. Arctic communities should benefit from tourism.
8. Trained staff are the key to responsible tourism.
9. Take the opportunity to learn about the Arctic.
10. Follow safety rules.

A tourist photographs a penguin chick in Antarctica.

FUTURE CHALLENGES

T he polar regions are a unique biome. The living things that can survive in them have adapted to an environment different from almost anywhere else on Earth. If the Arctic or Antarctic regions change significantly, many of the creatures that live in them will die out. They are not adapted to life in any other place.

Oil spills from a pipeline in Siberia. Oil leaks such as this are damaging the Arctic environment.

ENVIRONMENTAL CHALLENGES

Pollution is a major challenge for the future. The nations that fringe the Arctic now have cleaner industries than was the case 50 years ago. For example, PCBs are no longer widely used in industrial processes, and they were banned entirely in the U.S. in 1979. However, radioactive contamination and oil spills continue to affect the Arctic.

FACT FILE

POLLUTION LEVELS

A 2002 study commissioned by the U.S. Senate Environment and Public Works Committee assessed likely increases in pollution levels from fossil fuels:

• Electricity generation in the U.S. was forecast to increase 42 percent by 2020.

• Annual carbon dioxide emissions from power plants will rise nationwide by about 798 million tons (725 million t).

• Emissions of carbon dioxide will increase in all areas of the U.S., with a total increase of three percent.

Global warming is the major environmental challenge for both polar regions. No one is sure of the exact effect global warming will have on the polar ice, but there are already signs of it melting in unexpected places. If this continues, it will pose a global problem, with whole low-lying countries such as Bangladesh being flooded.

The difficulty is that the causes of global warming lie outside the Arctic, in the world's big industrial processes. Unless the world community decides to act together to halt temperature rises, progress is likely to be slow and inadequate.

HUMAN ISSUES

Another challenge for the Arctic is the culture of its people. It is becoming increasingly hard for native people to maintain anything like a traditional lifestyle. For example, only about 10 percent of Saami people still follow a traditional herding lifestyle. In Canada, Inuit people find it hard to keep up elements of their traditional hunting lifestyle: they cannot sell the furs of the animals they hunt because of a worldwide ban on seal-fur sales. On the positive side, Inuit people are able to have a far bigger say in governing their own affairs since the creation of their Nunavut homeland.

FACT FILE

THE ANTARCTIC

Global warming aside, the Antarctic faces fewer challenges than the Arctic:
• The Antarctic Treaty protects it from territorial disputes or commercial exploitation.
• The Antarctic is farther from regions with high human populations, as well as being far from major industrial centers, so it receives less pollution from outside.

Below: **Penguins dwarfed by a giant glacier.**

GLOSSARY

Baleen Also known as whalebone, baleen is comprised of sheets of horn-like material, the lower part fringed with bristles, that hang from the roof of the mouth of filter-feeding whales. It is used to strain plankton out of seawater. Whalebone formerly had several uses, including as stays in women's corsets.

Banishment Being sent away from a community to live elsewhere.

Biodiversity A wide range of different living things, adapted to a range of different environments.

Biome A region of Earth with a characteristic climate and type of vegetation, such as a desert, tropical forest, or wetland.

Cold War A state of tension between the two most powerful countries on Earth, the U.S. and the USSR. The Cold War began in the late 1940s and began to end in the late 1980s. The USSR broke apart in 1991, finally ending its rivalry with the U.S.

Concentrate To make stronger, usually by bringing together more of a particular thing. For example, an army might concentrate its forces on an enemy position by bringing more soldiers to fight in that particular place.

Contaminate To make impure or pollute.

Density The mass, or weight, of a substance in relation to its volume. Lead is denser than wood, for example, because a given volume of lead is heavier than the same volume of wood.

Extremities The fingers, hands, arms, toes, feet, legs, and head; the ends of the parts of the human body that are attached to the torso.

Food chain A group of interrelated living things that depend on one another for food, by eating one another. For example, plankton are eaten by fish, which are in turn eaten by seals, and seals are eaten by killer whales.

Fresh water Water from rain, which is not salty like seawater.

Graze To feed on growing grass or herbs.

Hibernation Spending winter in a state of deep sleep.

Icebreakers Ships that are specially equipped to break a path through icy seas.

Ice fishing Catching fish by dangling a line through a hole cut in the ice.

Igloo A temporary shelter made of blocks of ice and snow, used by Inuit hunters.

Income tax A tax (payment to the government) paid as a proportion of what someone earns.

Katabatic winds The movement of cold, dense air down a slope.

Kayaks Long, narrow boats with covered decks, paddled using a single oar that has a blade on each end.

Meltwater Water produced by melted snow or ice.

Migratory Moving from one place to another, usually in search of food.

Nomadic Living in different places at different times of the year, usually to make sure that herd animals have food. Nenets reindeer herders, for example, spend winter in the taiga forests and summer on the tundra.

Northern lights Streams and bands of light that appear in the night sky near the Arctic Circle. Also known as the aurora borealis.

Northwest Passage A route from Europe to Asia across or around northern North America. From 1524 to 1906, when Roald Amundsen completed the first voyage through the passage, navigators searched for such a route.

Organochlorines Long-lasting pesticides containing chlorine atoms that are used to control insects, normally to stop them from affecting crops.

Organophosphates Pesticides containing phosphorus atoms; they are not harmful to crops but can be extremely harmful to people and animals.

Over-fished When numbers of fish are reduced by so many that they are unlikely to recover.

PCBs (polychlorinated biphenyls) Chemicals that were once commonly used in industrial processes. Studies later showed that exposure to PCBs can cause birth defects, cancer, liver disorders, and nerve damage.

Permafrost The layer of soil in polar regions that remains frozen throughout the year.

Photosynthesize Manufacture sugars using light for energy.

Plateau A high, flat area of land.

Precipitation Rain, snow, sleet, fog, frost, dew, ice, or hail.

Self-contained Independent; not needing to take help or supplies from elsewhere.

Self-government A limited form of independence, where an area within a bigger country is given the right to make its own decisions about certain aspects of life.

Southern lights Streams and bands of light that appear in the night sky near the Antarctic Circle. Also known as the aurora australis.

Spermaceti A waxy material in the heads of sperm whales and bottlenose whales, which can be used to make candles. It is also used in some face creams, and as a lubricant.

Sub-Arctic Regions south of the Arctic where the summer temperature rises above 50 °F (10 °C), though not for more than four months of the year.

Umiaks Traditional Inuit boats covered mainly with skins. Umiaks are larger and wider than kayaks.

USSR Union of Soviet Socialist Republics, the country that from 1917 to 1991 controlled large areas of territory in Russia, eastern Europe, and northern and western Asia.

Walrus ivory Material from the tusks of male walrus.

Whale oil Oil taken from the blubber (rubbery flesh) of whales.

Wind chill A description of the effect the wind has on temperature. For example, a strong wind can make a warm day feel chilly, because it whips the heat away from a body.

WEB SITES TO VISIT

http://www.antarctica.ac.uk

This is the site of the British Antarctic Survey. It's even possible to get in contact with someone living in one of the Antarctic research stations.
British Antarctic Survey
High Cross, Madingly Road
Cambridge CB3 0ET, UK
E-mail: information@bas.ac.uk

http://www.spri.cam.ac.uk

The site of the Scott Polar Research Institute: not only a mine of useful information, but also a good place to find a very extensive links section to other polar sites.
Scott Polar Research Institute
University of Cambridge, Lensfield Road
Cambridge CB2 1ER, UK
E-mail: enquiries@spri.cam.ac.uk

http://www.mnh.si.edu/arctic

Site for the Smithsonian Institution's Arctic Studies Center, which focuses on the lives and history of northern peoples.
Arctic Studies Center
Department of Anthropology
National Museum of Natural History
Smithsonian Institution
Washington, D.C. 20560-0112
Tel: (202) 357-2682
E-mail: arctics@nmnh.si.edu

BOOKS TO READ

Baines, John D. *Antarctica*. Austin, Tex.: Raintree Steck-Vaughn, 1997.

Loewen, Nancy, and Ann Bancroft. *Four to the Pole*. North Haven, Conn.: Shoe String Press, 2001.

Taylor, Barbara. *Arctic and Antarctic*. New York: DK Publishing, 2000.

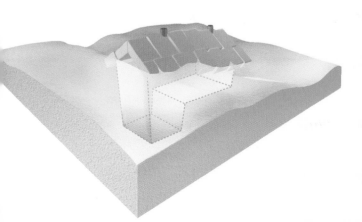

INDEX

Mason, Paul,
Polar regions /

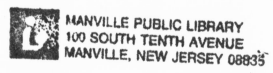
DEMCO